Catholic Churches
Big and Small

Stefan Salinas

Camelopardalis
SAN FRANCISCO

To my father,

Jimmy Salinas

A very, very busy
man of service

Special thanks to Jack Ronan, Rev. Thuan Hoang and Rev. Tony LaTorre
for their editing and ecclesiastical expertise.
   Additional help: Will Golden, Michael Somers, John Bollard and Rev. Steve Meriwether.
& Thanks to Bill Mathews for his support, and to Bill Dohar, the MHR Dysfunctional Coffee Group
and my family and friends for all of their love and encouragement.

Library of Congress Control Number: 2014907020
ISBN-10: 0692200886
ISBN-13: 9780692200889

Camelopardalis / Stefan Salinas, 2184 Sutter St. #275, San Francisco, CA 94115
www.stefansalinas.com
Printed in the U.S.A.

Have you ever been inside of a
Catholic church?

3

Thomas, Daddy and I are going to spend the day sketching churches with our teacher, Sister Barbara.

We say to her, "Good morning!"

Sister Barbara tells us that we celebrate mass in churches.

"We worship God and pray together," she says.

"And what else?"
Thomas asks.

She replies,

"Other special services are held inside, such as baptisms,

6

first communions, confirmations, weddings and funerals."

Churches are built in all sorts
of shapes.

9

Some have historic architecture,
busy with decorative
details,

while others are modern and simple.

Some are quite small.

Others are very, very tall.

15

All churches follow a basic floor plan.

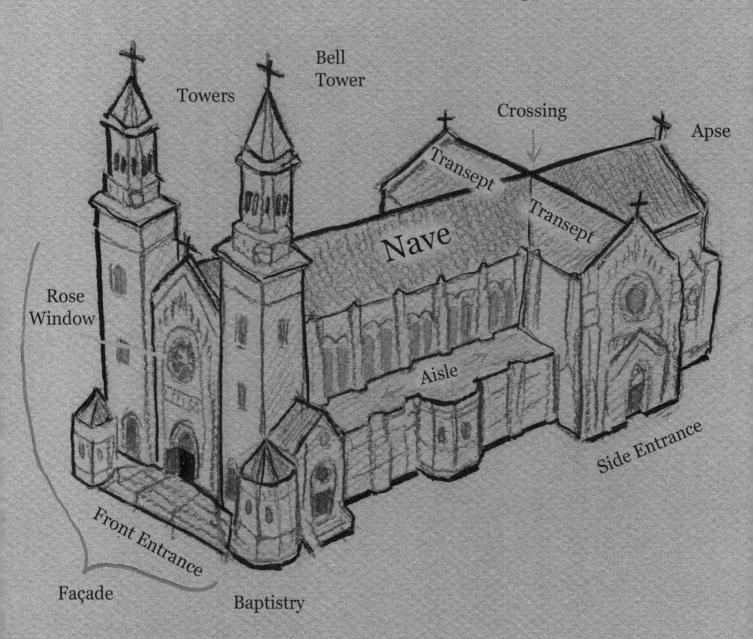

Towers

Bell
Tower

Crossing

Apse

Transept

Transept

Rose
Window

Nave

Aisle

Side Entrance

Front Entrance

Façade

Baptistry

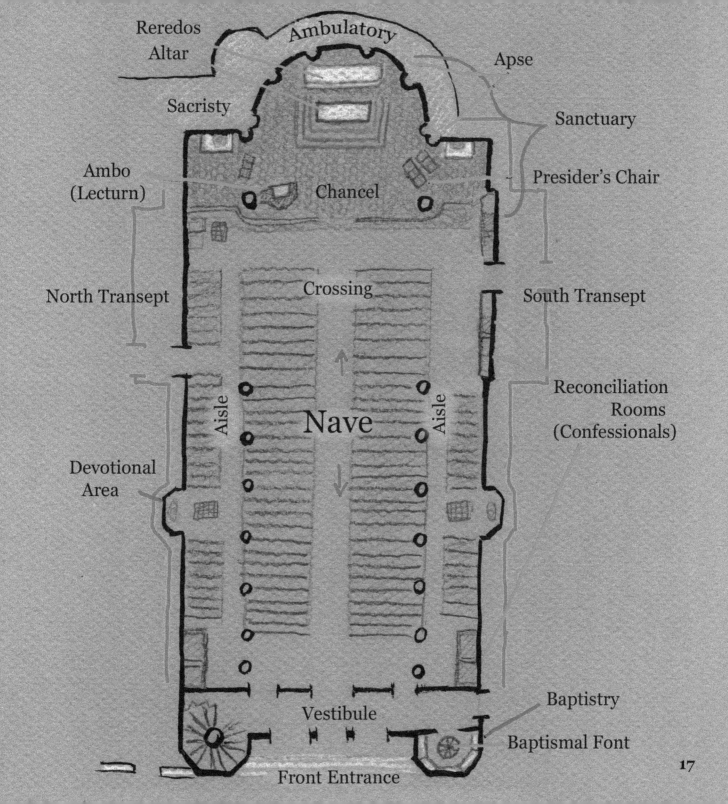

Reredos
Altar

Ambulatory

Apse

Sacristy

Sanctuary

Ambo
(Lecturn)

Presider's Chair

Chancel

North Transept

Crossing

South Transept

Aisle

Nave

Aisle

Reconciliation
Rooms
(Confessionals)

Devotional
Area

Baptistry

Vestibule

Baptismal Font

Front Entrance

17

Like houses, churches have furnishings.

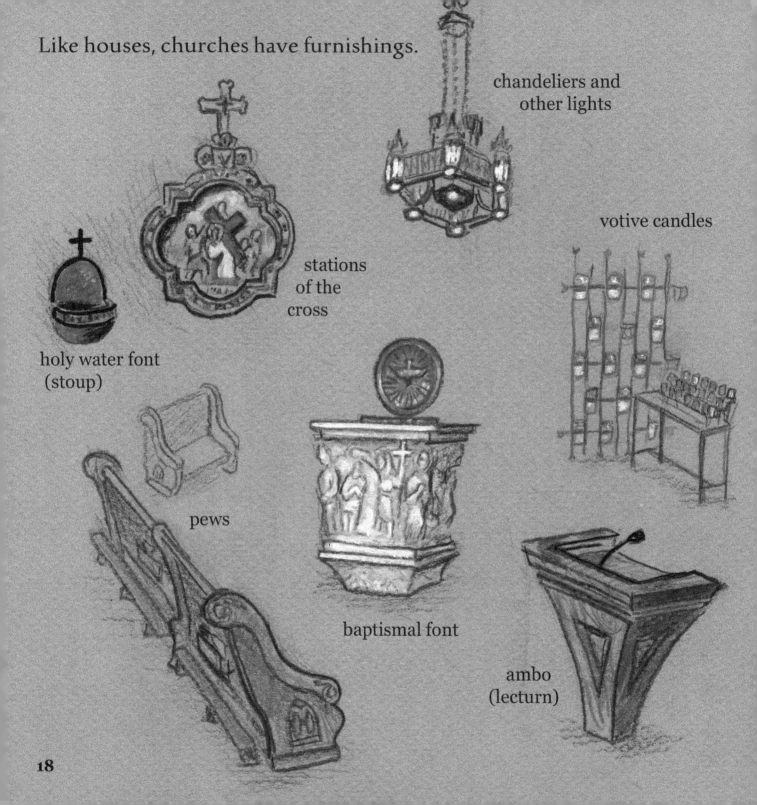

chandeliers and
other lights

votive candles

stations
of the
cross

holy water font
(stoup)

pews

baptismal font

ambo
(lectern)

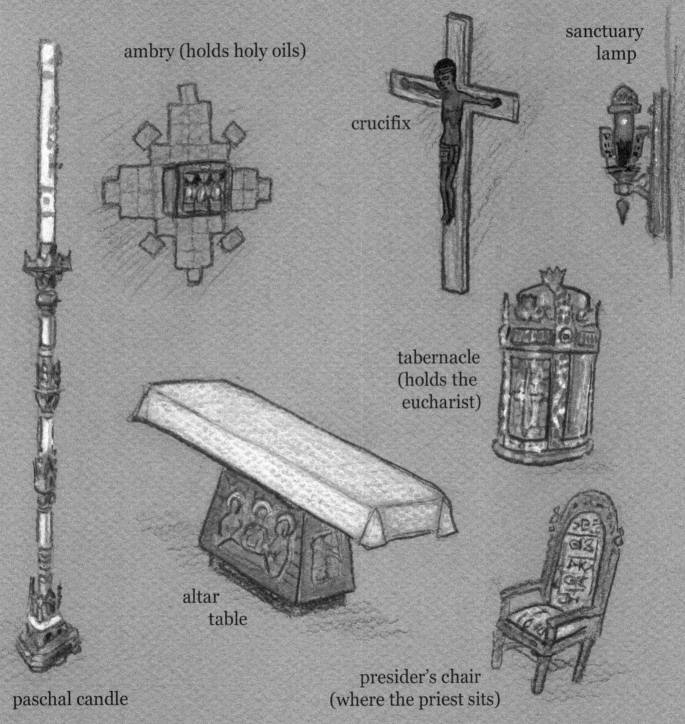

ambry (holds holy oils)

crucifix

sanctuary lamp

tabernacle (holds the eucharist)

altar table

paschal candle

presider's chair (where the priest sits)

19

We meet statues
of Jesus, saints
and angels...

21

...and see carvings
along the walls and
behind the altars.

23

Tapestries and
banners excite
our eyes,

and for our ears
there are organs:
keyboards connected
to large pipes.

The bell tower rings twelve times.
It's twelve o'clock, so we break
for lunch with Sister Cleta.

26

Back on tour, we see pictures made up of tiny tiles, called mosaics.
...And many pretty patterns greet us everywhere.

29

THIS BEGINNING OF MIRACLES DID
JESUS IN CANA

The sun's light enters
most beautifully through
stained glass windows.

30

THOU SHALT STRIKE

31

Scenes from
the Bible come
to life in murals
and paintings.

33

In the art, we find curious-looking symbols.

36

Some churches have mini-churches next to them, known as chapels.

Then there are side chapels: small chapels within churches.

Every diocese, or Catholic region,
has a head church, called a cathedral.
A large diocese is called
an archdiocese.

Throughout our tour, we have
seen the colors of the rainbow...

...along with many cultures
and traditions.

43

Sister Barbara tells us that   God is in churches,   God is outside,

God is everywhere...

45

God is also inside of you and me.

Whew! What a day!
We say good night to Sister Barbara as we drop her off,
then head for home.

The churches depicted in this book can be found within the Archdiocese of San Francisco, California.

CPSIA information can be obtained
at www.ICGtesting.com
Printed in the USA
LVHW020945241021
701343LV00002B/29